THE TALE OF HARRY THREE PAWS

Copyright notice

ISBN-13: 978-1542868907

Copyright © Marese Hickey 2018

All rights reserved. No part of this publication may be reproduced, translated, adapted, stored in a retrieval system or transmitted, in any form or by any means, including electronic, mechanical, photocopying, or recording without the prior written permission of the author, nor be otherwise circulated in any form of binding or cover other than that in which it is published and without a similar condition being imposed on the purchaser.

Cover Design: Marese Hickey

Cover Photo © Marese Hickey 2018

All photos in manuscript © Marese Hickey 2018

Editorial Team: Emma Champ, Sue Smith, Veron Bennett and Dolores O'Malley.

THE TALE OF HARRY THREE PAWS

Love, Angels and Cats with Cattitude

Marese Hickey

HTP Books

To Niall and Mary

Steadfast friends of Harry Three Paws

Prologue

Alice twisted and turned, needing sleep but unable to sleep for worrying about her beloved father in the next room. He was the same father as always but his body was failing. It was hard on him. Hard on everyone. Would she hear him ringing the bell if she fell asleep? She tried to think of something to calm her sore heart. She remembered how she had always cuddled a cat as a child needing comfort. She imagined a larger than life cat in her arms, purring, purring, purring...she drifted into sleep.

CHAPTER 1

Life before Harry Three Paws

Alice sped along on her bike to the next dog-walking job. The sky was open, blue and spacious. When she collected the dog, she suddenly decided that instead of turning right towards the park today, she would turn left towards the seafront. The little King Charles Cavalier was delighted with the new set of smells but there was a strange sound coming from the grass. Alice stopped, puzzled. She looked through the grass and found a lost black kitten, miaowing loudly in fear and anxiety. He looked like a little bat. She tucked him under her jacket and headed back. Should have him returned to his owners in a day or two, she thought confidently.

Six months later, Sid was particularly fond of jumping on her bare toes from under the bed and digging his claws in. This resulted in a lot of swearing and one-footed hopping around. Still, it was hard to stay angry at the whirlwind of long black fur streaking down the stairs with his big tail in the air. It made her laugh. She could do with laughing. Since her Dad had died earlier in the year, her heart had felt heavy with grief and empty with loss.

Sid

My full name is Sidney Divilskin. Once upon a time, I was playing with my brothers and sisters and friends. We were in the Golden Field where you go between cat-on-earth-lives. It's beautiful. There are caretakers there and they really love animals. You never feel hungry or afraid. Big cousin cats like lions and tigers stroll around but never hurt us. There are dogs too, and they are so relaxed they don't chase us. Everyone has a full belly, a beautiful bed to snuggle into, friends to play with, and nothing to do all day except play and sleep and eat. The sun always shines and there is no darkness or cold rain. I was going to say it's like heaven but of course it IS heaven. Because we are in spirit, we eat vegetarian cat food. On earth of course, that would be no good because we need a special ingredient called taurine, only found in meat, to keep our heart muscle healthy.

Anyway, there I was, romping around and chasing my friend Isabella. We were playing a game of tag. I would hide, and then Isabella had to find me and we would roll around and play fight. Then she would lick my head because she really loved me. She was licking my head when an angel appeared. We all got very quiet in a respectful way. The angels are lovely. They are really shiny and the love just pours out of them. I watched carefully to see who the angel was going to call and I was really gobsmacked when it was me. Me! An ordinary cat! The angel picked me up very gently and petted me. I purred loudly. She said she had a special mission for me. It would involve me going back to earth for a lifetime. I was needed. She said I was free to agree to go or not. There was no problem if I didn't want to go because I already knew that incarnating was a tough choice. She said I could think about it, talk to my family and friends about it and she would come back tomorrow.

When she left, all my family and friends crowded around me, whispering "What did she say? What did she say?" I explained the situation. Isabella turned and walked away, her head down. She knew I wouldn't refuse an angel, even though I would be leaving her behind.

When the angel came back the next day, there was a nice man with her. He had the brightest of bright blue eyes and a kind smile. The angel picked me up and the man petted me gently on the head. He whispered in my ear what he wanted me to do. He and the angel looked at me. I said Yes.

On earth I was born into a family of four kittens. The family didn't want us kittens and they deliberately drowned three of my brothers. I felt very scared and I could feel the grief and sadness of my furry cat mammy. She was down to one kitten now.

When I was about three months old, the man in the family put me in the car on a stormy November night and drove down the causeway towards his golf club. He stopped the car, picked me up by the scruff and threw me away. I was terrified of the noise of the thunder and lightning. The rain was torrential. I didn't know where I was or what was happening. I wanted my cat mammy.

Exhausted, I eventually I fell asleep in the wet grass.

The next morning, I was freezing, hungry and afraid. I started miaowing loudly to try to get help. I could see humans walking past but no one stopped. Then there was a woman with a small dog. She heard me and stopped. She searched through the grass and found me. When she picked me up, something stirred in my memory but I couldn't hold on to it.

She put me under her jacket where it was warm and brought me back to the dog's house. The dog was gentle and friendly if a bit confused as to what I was doing there. That made two of us because I was so cold and hungry I didn't know what was going on. The woman said she would come back to collect me in her car. I was terrified at the sound of that because of being thrown out of the car the previous night. She came back with a cage, put me in it, and wrapped up me up in a warm blanket. She covered the cage with another blanket and I felt a bit safer then. When we got back to her place, she gave me food and then took photos of me. She said I was such a beautiful puddy cat that I must have gotten lost during the storm. She said she was sure that she could get me reunited with my family within a couple of days. If only she knew.

She brought me to Denis the vet who checked me out. He called the woman Alice. He said I had no microchip, fleas or diseases and it was safe to bring me to her home.

After a couple of days in the new place, I began to look around me. There was a very, very old cat living there. Her name was Gannet. She was black and white and only had one ear which was very sore looking. When I saw her, again, something stirred on the fringes of my memory, but I couldn't remember what.

Alice couldn't find my family because of course they definitely weren't looking for me. She sighed and said she guessed that she was my new Cat Mammy. When I settled in, I began chasing her up and down the stairs and jumping on her bare toes from under the bed. That made her laugh, but it was a strange sound. It was like it was rusty. If I went into the room where Gannet was, Alice didn't like it at all. She didn't want the old cat upset. Gannet was dying. I could see that. We animals always know.

Gannet

There were three parts to my life's work with Mammy. My first job was to teach her patience and perseverance. As I was a feral cat, this bit was easy. Every time she opened the door I ran and hid. It took her six months to move my food dish up near the back door and two years before I allowed her to pat me on the head.

Once she came home to find me sitting on the neighbour's front doorstep. As I was such a scaredy cat, this was highly unusual. The neighbour asked Mammy to remove me as she didn't like cats. Mammy could see I was sick but at that time there was no nearby vet and she had no car. She examined my fur and saw that someone had put flea powder on me. She rightly guessed that it was flea powder for dogs, which is toxic to cats. In desperation, she filled a basin with warm water and coconut oil shampoo, and lifted me into it. It was a measure of how sick I was that I allowed her to do it. She dried me off and put me lying on a hot water bottle beside a warm radiator. I survived and got better.

After that, our relationship changed and I began to trust her. It was just as well because we ended up spending eighteen years together.

I believe that some people called me a bit odd but you know that is their problem. I had a liking for sleeping in strange places. Mammy seemed to find it very funny that I would sleep on top of a thorn bush or on top of a small flower pot with most of me spilling off each side.

Sometimes she would put on a dance DVD supposed to be for getting fit and losing weight. She would dance around the place and I would join her. I would wind in and out through her legs which made things more interesting for both of us. I especially enjoyed the Lindy Hop. I also liked when she used to hang out the washing. On those occasions I used to emerge from under the bushes to interact with the peg box. Mammy said the box was my friend Peg. (And they said that I was the eccentric one!)

In later years, I got both kidney failure and cancer on my ears. By this time there was a local vet, called Denis. I was put on tablets and one of my ears was removed. It was just the outer flap so I didn't really mind.

Mammy brought me to a healer to see could he help with the other ear which wasn't too bad. I was aghast. I spent ages in the car wherever she drove me, and when we got there the man had four dogs in his kitchen and I nearly died of fright. I had never even been close to a dog before. Mammy held me on her knee and then something really strange happened. Even though I was petrified of the new situation, stressed by the journey and terrified of the dogs, I started to relax. By the time he finished I was like a jelly cat. It was like my bones had turned to mush. I couldn't be bothered being afraid, I was too chilled out.

Mammy made an appointment for a second visit. It never happened because I hid and she couldn't catch me. I heard her on the phone to the healer, apologising for cancelling the appointment. She said with a laugh that she would have to learn this healing business herself. I purred to myself under the bushes. Phase Two of my life's mission was underway. Sure enough, Mammy became an energy healer. The angels had been right – she would not have done it for herself. But she did it for me. We spent many long months on the sofa together, with me sitting on her feet while she gave me healing. She showed me a cartoon once of a skeleton with a cat sitting on its knee. The caption was "Because she didn't want to disturb the cat." "That's you and me, Gan," she said, and when she did get up she hobbled around until she could walk.

I was ready to go into spirit for a long time before it happened. Mammy's father was sick and she told me she couldn't bear to lose both of us at the same time. I was philosophical about it. When the time came, she asked Denis the vet to help me let go of my worn-out fur body. But I can see that this is a hard thing for humans to do. It is hard to kill the thing you love. Humans create great suffering for themselves by holding on too long and too tightly. We animals love life but we remember where we came from and where we are going back to. We know that we are made of unconditional love like everything else in the universe. We know that we will be met by an angel at the

Rainbow Bridge and that one day we will be reunited with our loved ones. We know it for sure. So we don't see death like humans do. We see beyond it, to what is real. To be loved and accepted exactly as you are is unconditional love. And unconditional love is the only real thing in the world.

Sid

I was there six months when things went downhill for Gannet. New Cat Mammy slept on the floor beside her on the last night. Denis the vet came to the house. He was very kind. He gave Gannet an injection and she passed into spirit, purring against New Cat Mammy's heart. To this day I'm still not sure if she died because of what the vet gave her or if she was drowned by tears. I came in and sniffed the body but Gannet and I hadn't been friends so I wasn't upset. New Cat Mammy was distraught.

That night, she twisted and turned in bed, exhausted but unable to sleep. I crept up on her bed and nudged her with my head. She lifted the duvet and I went in underneath it. Then out again, in again, out again, in again, purring loudly with my large furry tail in the air. I lay down and started kneading the inside of Mammy's arm with my front claws. She covered my claws with a small fleece blanket so that she wouldn't be like Shredded Wheat. Finally satisfied, I settled down close to her heart and purred long and loud with my big bass purr rumbling through her chest.

I had remembered at last. The man with blue eyes had said that Gannet would be passing into spirit and that I was needed to bring comfort. It was what I came here to do. New Cat Mammy became just Mammy then, because the love bonded us together. She remembered imagining a big furry cat to hug when her heart was sore. She smiled and relaxed. "Thanks Sid. Thanks Dad," she whispered, as she drifted into sleep.

In the summertime there is a white rambling rose in the back garden. It smells nice. Every morning Mammy goes out and dead heads the rose. Then she scatters the soft petals over Old Gannet's grave. "This is for you, Gannet," she says. People believe that boundaries are very definite but they are more porous than you might think. In the Golden Field, I know that Gannet – who now has a perfect fur body – feels the beautiful rose petals showering down on her like angel's feathers. I saw it when I was there. There are no barriers to love. It lasts forever.

A few months after Gannet went over the Rainbow Bridge into the Golden Field, Mammy came home from Dog's Aid with a cat basket. This looked ominous. She put the new cat in a cage in the sitting room and covered it with a blanket. I sniffed around. It was a strange smell. It reminded me of something or someone. Mammy said the new arrival was going to be called Izzy after a comedian called Eddie Izzard. I have no idea of the inner workings of the human brain.

After a day or two, I snuck into the sitting room while Mammy was cleaning the litter tray. I stopped dead, and then ran up to the cage. Izzy jumped down off the cat basket and we bumped noses through the bars. "Well, well. Friends already," said Mammy, not knowing how right she was. She opened the cage door. Izzy, formerly Isabella, strolled out of the cage and licked me on the head. We were reunited. I was delighted. When I had volunteered for this mission, I didn't know that my play buddy and soul mate Isabella would be joining me. After that, whenever I came in from my wanderings, Izzy would jump down from her perch on the windowsill and run to greet me. We were delighted to be able to play and grow up together.

Old Gannet had been the only cat in the house for eighteen years. Mammy never wanted to upset her by bringing home permanent cats. After Gannet went into spirit, Mammy lost the run of herself and brought home yet another cat. That would make three of us – me, Izzy and now this one. He was a three legged tabby called Harry Three Paws. He had a bad attitude and I didn't like him. When I saw what happened between him and my soul mate Izzy, I was proved right. She was always a happy cat until Harry came along.

CHAPTER 2

The Arrival of Harry Three Paws

I'm Harry. When I was born, I was an ordinary kitten with four paws. I had a nice home and I loved being an Only Cat, not one cat of many. The children loved me and I loved them. They put a tinsel crown on my head and called me Prince Harry. I knocked it off with my paw and ate it, but I felt like royalty all the same. I had a great time playing with the children, chasing strings and feathers and pouncing on anything that moved. I thought the world was my oyster, exciting, bright and fun. One morning I ran out the front door into the road, eager to explore this amazing new world of space. I never heard the car coming.

When I was hit by the car, they brought me to the vet who said he could save me but not my leg. My family said they would be mortified to have a cat with only three legs and that people would be laughing at them. They told the vet to put me asleep and that they would get a new cat. They meant that they wanted me killed. When I heard that I was terrified.

I was in a lot of pain already because my leg was in bits but then my heart broke into bits too. I had thought that they loved me but they were prepared to throw me away like I was a piece of rubbish. That hurt me even more than my mangled leg. People think that animals don't have feelings, but we do. We feel love and hope, fear and rejection. We have dreams of being loved and cherished.

When I woke up the next day, my leg, home and family were all gone. I was in shock and felt dazed by the way my life had changed so profoundly in an instant. I felt hurt, angry and rejected. As the weeks went by, I felt ashamed of my body because my balance was gone and my spine was sore from trying to get around on three legs. Sometimes I overbalanced and I was very embarrassed. I used to be so graceful, and I took it all for granted.

I ended up in an animal shelter called Dog's Aid in Dublin. It's not a posh place but it's a good place. It's run by a woman called Maggie. Maggie smells good, like a cat but with a lot of dog thrown in. Helen runs the cattery and she was very kind to me.

One day I was resting and a woman came into the cattery. She had an appalling fashion sense and was wearing some kind of orange outfit like I had once seen on a television program about a prison. However, I could see her energy and it was soft. Not all animals can see the colours around people and other animals, but I can. Some animals sense the energy instead of seeing it. I could see this woman had good heart energy, nice and pink and green.

Someone came in and asked her how the healing was going and I understood then that she was an animal healer. I granted her the privilege of sitting on her knee and allowed her to give me Reiki healing energy. It felt warm, safe, comforting and relaxing. It eased the discomfort in my spine. I snoozed, and when I woke, I looked up at her and used CMT - the Cat Manipulation Technique that all cats are born knowing about. It's called the Silent Miaow and it goes straight to the human heart. It's a bit unfair, but hey, so is life, as I had recently discovered. It took a couple of weeks but sure enough, one day my healer brought me home with her. She said this was my new forever home and that I would always be minded and loved here. I took that with a pinch of salt.

When I began to settle in to my new home, I took stock. It was warm. It was safe. My New Mammy seemed kind, but there was a problem. Actually, there were two problems. One was called Izzy and the other was called Sid. Izzy was a tuxedo cat, black with a white shirt. Sid was a huge big black furry thing. Neither of them was pleased to see me, and I was horrified to see them!

When I used the Silent Miaow on potential New Mammy, it didn't occur to me that she already had cats. Why would she invite me, Prince Harry, to share accommodation with other plebs? I was distraught, because New Mammy clearly did not understand me at all. I wanted things to be the way they used to be. I wanted my leg back. And especially, I wanted to be An Only Cat.

Izzy had also come from Dog's Aid, a few months before me. She was of feral origin. She was the same age as me, and I hated her. I hated her because she had four legs, and New Mammy used to call her My Feral Girl and My Sweet Pussycat Angel in a special, soft voice. Izzy had been abandoned as a kitten with her siblings on a construction site. Many feral cats that become tame are very happy to stay inside because they know what it's like to live on the street. It's a case of "Been there, done that, no thank you!"

Izzy spent a lot of time in her comfortable bed on the window sill. She loved Sid and the two of them were friends.

Every time Sid came inside Izzy would jump down and go over to greet him with her tail in the air. She was always pleased to see him. She often walked around with her tail straight up in the air - until I came along. I started chasing her. I had this anger, hurt and rage inside me and it's like it pushed me around - so I pushed her around. Nothing New Mammy did made any difference and she tried everything: time-outs for me in a different room, extra healing Reiki, flower essences and this diffuser thing that smelled like a mother cat's pheromones. I shredded New Mammy a lot too. Pretty soon Izzy's tail went down and stayed down. That should have made me happy but it didn't. Nothing could.

After nearly six months, I began to feel a bit better and stopped chasing her so much. One day I was having a nap on the window sill, in what used to be Izzy's basket. I had commandeered it. I had been up for two hours so I was due a nap after a heavy morning. I was unceremoniously awoken when some cat launched a surprise attack on me. I rolled over to protect myself, expecting to see Sid, even though he was usually peaceful and because he was so big, I had never chased him. I may have lost a leg in the accident but I didn't get a bang on the head that made me stupid. Instead, I had been attacked by docile little Izzy!

It made me look at her a different way and after that, I stopped hassling her. She hadn't hurt me when she attacked. The only thing that was hurt was my pride, because New Mammy saw what happened and she fell about the place laughing and said "Good girl Izzy."

The local vet is called Denis. I suppose he's okay but obviously I'm not at my best when we meet. New Mammy reckons I am intent on single pawedly reflating the Irish economy through visits to Denis. Denis says

I'm uninsurable and I'll bet he said some unrepeatable things about me after my last visit. I had hurt my leg again running away from a dog, so even though he didn't catch me I was very sore. Denis was very sore too after I shredded him with The Claw. The Claw is a weapon of mass destruction I engineered to make up for my missing back leg. I file The Claw daily on Mammy's sea grass chair (or what's left of it.) It doesn't always protect me but it's the best I can do.

The first time a dog caught me here in the street outside my new home, I was in a lot of pain. I found it hard to breathe. New Mammy rushed me to Denis who gave me a general anaesthetic. I was terrified that she was going to have me put to sleep or give me away, because after all, my first time at a vet was not a happy occasion. But New Mammy had a break in her voice as she said to Denis to do whatever he needed to make me better and she would find the money. I needed seventeen stitches. Denis said I was lucky to survive, that the dog nearly punctured my lung, but I love life and I never give up. New Mammy says if she could bottle my spirit she'd be a millionaire. After that day, I was able to believe that New Mammy really wanted me and would not betray me, so even though it really hurt to have been in the jaws of that dog, something good came out of it. I was able to relax a bit. I started calling her just Mammy then.

When I had my accident and lost my leg, my family and my home, my guardian angel whispered soft words of comfort into my ear but I turned away and fired her for inefficiency. Why had she not saved me from being hit by the car? I told her I wanted nothing more to do with her. Angels can only help us if we ask. They can't impose their help on us. Some people think that cats have neither souls nor guardian angels but they are wrong. Of course we do - why wouldn't we? Humans can be so arrogant. I can see angels as well as the colours around living things. My angel was upset to be sent away and I could see her drooping but I hardened my heart. Life was tough and I had to be tough too, to survive.

When the rage inside me started to burn out, my angel started whispering soft words to me that sounded like Mammy's Izzy voice.

One day I was in a dream state between sleep and waking and my guard was down. She whispered in my ear: You are creating your own suffering by holding on to anger and bitterness, when love is right here where you are. I shook my head to make the words go away, but they were inside me now.

I didn't want to change because like all cats, I hate change, but the next day, the sun was shining and I ran out onto the front lawn where Mammy was weeding the flower bed. I could see Mammy looking at me keenly, sensing a change in me. Words kept running through my head, and I don't know if they were mine or my angel's but maybe it didn't matter. They said: Stop whining - the world doesn't owe you a leg. Mourn your losses then tear the moss up. So I did. I tore the moss up from the front lawn. It felt good and besides, it made Mammy laugh. She pointed to a spot and said, "I think you missed a bit there, Harry." Eventually I reinstated my guardian angel but I told her to up her game if she wanted to keep her job.

☼

Spring arrived and Mammy was out in the back garden. It was a sunny but windy day. All of us cats love the wind because it energises us, and we were all dashing around like crazy. Mammy was sowing seed potatoes and I was supervising, doing quality control. She would put them in the earth and I would hook them back out with The Claw. Then I would chase them around the garden, playing Spudball. She took off the lid of the compost bin and put it on the ground. I inserted The Claw and I got in under the lid. I am highly skilled at such manoeuvres, which often surprises people. When she tapped on it I stuck The Claw out underneath the lid and Mammy laughed out loud. I like that sound. Mammy says I am a natural comedian.

Sid meanwhile was on the swing seat, swinging himself back and forth like Mrs Bates in "Psycho" as he chewed on a raspberry cane. Izzy was toying with worms that had been under a compost bag, and then I helped her by tearing a new opening in the bag to examine the contents. Mammy threw her eyes up to heaven but said we were all a GREAT help in the garden and that she'd be lost without us.

One day a man arrived with a new back door that had a cat flap in it. I supervised him putting it in, of course, to make sure he did it right. Mammy opened the flap and we sniffed it suspiciously. I sat on one side of it and Sid sat on the other. I batted it gently with my paw. Then I punched it with my paw and it flew up and hit Sid in the face. He was furious but I was thrilled! I immediately saw that whoever took charge of the flap was in charge of cat comings and goings. Naturally, that person was me.

Izzy, being a feral cat, was very cautious about the new flap. Mammy posted her out through it and then went to the other side to give her a treat. A while later, Mammy would post her back in and give her a treat. This went on for three weeks before Izzy got the hang of it. Or perhaps she had copped on a lot earlier and pretended not to understand in order to get more treats. That's what I should have done, but sometimes I'm too smart for my own good. Izzy probably didn't have that level of deviousness in her anyway. She had had a tough start in life but was happy to be in love with Sid and to be able to play with him. Her needs were simple.

Mammy foolishly thought that once the horrendously expensive cat flap was installed, her days of opening and closing doors were over. Not so. Sid took to sitting on the front window sill when he couldn't be bothered going around the back to use the cat flap. And naturally we often wanted Mammy to open the door to maintain her door skills. She is generally very patient but in wintertime an edge of steel would enter her voice as we vacillated in the doorway with the expensive heat going out and the polar air coming in. "In or out now!" Those who couldn't decide were helped by a gentle toe on the furry bum, much to our disgruntlement. It's SO hard to find good help these days.

Chapter 3

More Cats

Tilly

I had been dumped in a doorway of a shop during the snow, and when the snow melted I nearly drowned. All I remember was being very frightened. I couldn't breathe. The water was so cold. I felt panic as the water came up over my head. Then someone lifted me up by the scruff and I froze because that is my instinct. It wasn't my furry mammy though. She was gone and I never saw her or my brothers or sisters again. I ended up in Dog's Aid, an animal sanctuary that takes cats too. I got pneumonia and had to have an injection. Once I started feeling better, I looked around me and I could see that this was an okay place. I am a feral cat, which means my brain is wired differently to other cats. I take no chances when it comes to humans. My motto is Run and Hide. Or it used to be. Because everyone in Dog's Aid cattery was so nice to me, I gradually got used to being around humans. I began to believe that they could be kind.

There was a woman called Rita there and she was very calm and kind to all of us cats. One day, I was back in a cage again because I needed more antibiotics for yet another chest infection. This weird woman (not Rita) came in wearing strange orange clothes. She came up to my cage and of course I hid inside my basket. I could see out through the slits in it though. I saw her putting her hands on the outside of my basket and I tensed, ready to panic. Then something odd happened. I started to feel heat coming from her hands. Eventually I relaxed. She stopped after a few minutes and moved on to another cage where she did the same thing.

The following week she came again but I was better so I was out of the cage. She sat down on an old sofa and the heat started coming out of her hands. I couldn't help myself, I sidled up to her. I wanted more of that cosy, Mammy-cat type feeling. I even let her touch me on the top of my head with one finger, and I didn't attack her. Over the next few months, she would sit on the sofa and I got more and more confident. I would let her rub me and I liked it.

One day I heard the cattery people talking. There was going to be a new cattery. It would mean that all the cats had to be fostered (whatever that was) so that the old portacabin could be scrapped to make way for the new cattery. I felt tense. I knew this meant change. Cats don't like change. In that sense, our cat brains are all wired the same way.

Anyway, one day the Orange Woman sat on the sofa and the heat started coming from her hands as usual. I came up for my admiration and she caught me by the scruff of the neck. I was so shocked I froze. She stuffed me in a basket and put me in her car. She explained that I was going to stay in her house for a while and then I would be coming back as there would be a lovely new cattery for us cats. I was in a cage for two weeks in her sitting room and I could see two other cats. The Top Cat was a big black furry thing called Sid. I'm not much into romance but I'm not blind either. He was very handsome. You wouldn't kick him out of your cat bed for having fleas.

The other was a disabled cat with only three legs called Harry. I vaguely remembered seeing him in the cattery when I was a kitten. He was a tabby like me, and it was a bit confusing. It was like looking in the mirror and seeing myself with only three legs. I wouldn't like that. I wouldn't like that at all. I am a ferocious Hunter Cat. A missing leg would be a disaster for me. I was quite bored in the cage but the Orange Woman fed me well. One day I heard her talking to a friend who was visiting. She said that the cattery building had been delayed and she felt bad about keeping me in a cage. Her friend said "I guess you could let her out, and then when the cattery is built, bring her back." So the Orange Woman let me out. She hasn't taken me back to the cattery yet. It's been four years so maybe I can relax now.

☼

Harry Three Paws

One day I came home from my travels and neighbourhood supervision to find Mammy setting up a cage in the sitting room. This did not look good. Sure enough, what emerged from a cat basket only Yet Another Cat. This one was called Tilly. To add insult to injury, she was a tabby like me. In fact, we were so alike she could have been my doppelganger. The only way you could tell us apart is that she had four legs and I only have three. Also, she was a mad feral, not a tame feral like Izzy.

Mammy said Tilly had got attached to her because she nearly drowned as a kitten in the bad winter and had needed so much Reiki in Dog's Aid. Allegedly she was just staying while the Dog's Aid cattery was being done up. Yeah, right. No prize for figuring out how that plan went. Eventually Tilly settled down and when she did, she started eating for Ireland. She ate her own food, Sid's food, my food and the general food. She grew bigger and bigger.

Mammy started calling her The Lynx and she did indeed resemble that cousin of ours. She and Sid quickly became friends and they would chase each other up and down the stairs. Mammy said cats were supposed to be quiet, not like two horses. Sometimes Mammy would lift her up and swing her around and go "Whee! Look, the first feral cat in space!" and Tilly loved it. Sid would get jealous as he was Top Cat. (I had no interest in being Top Cat as I just wanted to be Only Cat. But I'm sure I could have been Top Cat if the position arose because I certainly have the brains for it.) Then Mammy would play with Sid and sing "Who's got Sidney's kidney?" to cheer him up. It always worked because he idolised her.

Sid is special to Mammy because she believes that her beloved father sent him to her from the world of spirit. I know this is true because I asked my angel and she said yes, that is what happened. When Sid cuddles up to Mammy (all eleven pounds of him) I see her sending pink love to him that goes from the top of his ears to the tip of his tail. He sends her love too, so they both are encompassed in a soft pink cloud of furry love.

Humans have this weird idea that cats can be owned. It's not true of course. I am my own cat. Mammy says I'm like a teenager as I only come home to eat and drop off my furry washing. I visit at least two sets of neighbours every day and try to be even-pawed about gracing them with my presence.

Mammy says I have a bit of obsessive compulsive disorder or OCD. I don't know what OCD is but I do know that I feel agitated if I don't stick to my routine. I like to depart from my back door at 08:25 and be at Niall and Mary's house by 08:27. I stand up on my one back leg and place my muddy two front paws on their sparkling clean glass door. I do the Silent Miaow. Now, people would have to be very hard-hearted to resist a three-legged cat AND a Silent Miaow. Niall and Mary are not in the least bit hard-hearted. Niall gets up from his chair to let me in and I immediately shoot past him and hop up onto his nice warm chair. He has to move elsewhere then but that is his problem. I stay with them for hours and leave when it suits me. They admire me and tell me I'm a beautiful boy. They have a special cushion on an upstairs chair just for me. In their house, I am The Only Cat. It's nice to be appreciated.

One day they went off and another neighbour was minding their house. I rocketed in past him and he didn't see me because of my tabby camouflage in the dark. He locked me in by mistake and nearly had a heart attack the next day when he came in and there I was, calmly sitting on the stairs.

He flew upstairs to see had I made a mess but of course I had not. I am an impeccable cat with amazing bladder retention. The only sign I had left behind me was a dent in each bed because I had tested them all to see which was the most comfortable. When Niall told Mammy this she said I was like Goldilocks trying out the beds and they both laughed.

My next stop down the line is Mona, Julian and Maeva. They absolutely adore me. There was a fly in the ointment for a while because they got their own cat (whatever that means) called Simba. When he was a kitten he loved having me sharing his space but when he got older, not so much. I got edged out. A few months ago, though, he disappeared. I swear I had nothing to do with it. I waited a whole twenty-four hours before flying in their front door like a projectile missile and up to the main bedroom. I took my rightful place in the centre of the biggest bed. It was good to be back.

Like many cats, I am curious, and personally I have a fascination with ladders. They always seem to lead somewhere that requires exploration. I'm just a cat who can't say no to ladders. You might think that the absence of a fourth leg would cramp my style but no way! When I was younger I used to do a corkscrew upwards ascent on the local trees. My descent was less graceful but got the job done.

Niall had a ladder against his house one day as he was cleaning his windows. Now, Mammy is great but this is not something I've ever seen her do. Sometimes she cleans her upstairs windows from the inside but of course there's no excitement in that for me. And it's fairly rare anyway. She says that no-one ever lay on their deathbed and said, "I wish I had done more housework." I heard her on the phone to her friend Maeve one day, who apparently found herself dusting behind a radiator and immediately rang

Mammy to make an arrangement to meet for an emergency lunch.

Another day I came back inside to find a strange, elongated table in the kitchen. I jumped up on it and it rocked a bit. When Mammy came into the kitchen she cracked up laughing. "Do you like the ironing board, Harry?" she asked. Whatever it was for, I only saw it that one time and never since.

Anyway, back to the ladder. Niall went inside to get something and up the ladder I went. It was quite high and very exciting. He called Mary out and the two of them were laughing, presumably with me and not at me, as they are my friends after all. Niall took a photo of me, and as I turned to pose for the camera I lost my balance and fell, bouncing off his car bonnet and sliding onto the ground. I shook myself and did a quick groom of my left shoulder to fend off embarrassment, and stalked off as best as I could on three legs.

On another occasion I went upstairs at home and there was a ladder going up into the attic that had not been there when I left at 08:25. Naturally I immediately ascended to check out the situation. I sniffed the insulation and the swing seat cushions and turned to come back down. Unfortunately, it became immediately apparent that I just couldn't do it without falling. Mammy came up carrying a spare foam mattress and shook her head when she saw me. "Stay there," she said, and came back five minutes later with a rucksack. She put me into it, closed it, and put it on her back as she climbed downstairs. She took a photo when I emerged from the backpack with my skeleton intact but my dignity dented.

Another day I went into a neighbour's garden in the usual way but when I went to leave, an element of my outward bound route (garden chair, bin, oil tank) had been changed and I couldn't get out again. I usually have an Inward Bound Route and a different Outward Bound Route. It wasn't possible to use the Inward Bound Route to get out. I don't normally say much (I'm more of an observer than a talker) but eventually I had to start miaowing loudly.

Niall heard me (which was good because Mammy is as deaf as a post) and said, "Don't worry, Harry, we'll get you out." He sat on the back wall at the end of his garden and slid his ladder over the wall, and Mammy used the ladder to climb in and carry me out. Then she handed the ladder back to Niall who handed it down to Mary in their garden. Half the neighbourhood were out helping, sitting on walls, moving ladders and giving advice! One lady came out with her glass of wine. It was quite convivial. I felt a bit ruffled but Mammy didn't make a big thing of it. She just said I was lucky to be a Community Cat and that we were lucky her knee hadn't given out on the ladder because she wasn't getting any younger. At least she didn't put me in a rucksack. If she had done that I would have expired of pure mortification!

CHAPTER 4

Hard Times

Harry Three Paws

One morning Mammy staggered in the front door with Izzy in her arms. There was a sound coming out of Mammy that I had never heard from her before, but I knew instantly what it was. I recognised it from my own heart. It was grief and loss. Izzy looked to be asleep but there was no colour around her and I knew she was dead. Her spirit was gone. She had been hit by a car. Mammy sat on the back doorstep rocking Izzy back and forth in her arms, with grief pouring out of her eyes and mouth and energy field. She didn't know I was behind her when she whispered in Izzy's ear that she was sorry that I had made her short life a misery. My heart sank when I heard that. I knew that Izzy had gone over the Rainbow Bridge and was fine in spirit, but even so, I felt a bit guilty.

☼

Sid

At that time, Mammy used to allow us to be outside during the night time. We cats are nocturnal, so we were thrilled. One night I was out the back of the house while Izzy was out the front. I came in late and went to bed for my beauty sleep.

The next morning Mammy nearly fell in the door with Izzy in her arms. There was a wave of grief and horror coming from Mammy. She eventually showed me Izzy, whose fur body was dead. I nearly leaped out of my fur with the shock. I hid under the bed. My friend Izzy! She was dead. She had only been with me for a year. Gone into spirit without me. I was broken hearted.

Harry Three Paws

Eventually Mammy got to her feet and found a cardboard box. She took out a soft pink blanket with hearts on it and wrapped Izzy gently in it, like she was still alive. She put her favourite toy mouse beside her and pinned an angel figurine to the blanket. It took ages for her to dig a grave at the bottom of the garden. When it was all done Mammy went inside and got into bed even though it was daytime. She pulled the blankets over her head to muffle her crying. Sid was freaked out and gutted that his love friend was gone forever and wasn't coming back. Mammy was lying on her side, curled into a ball. I crept in beside her and started purring. It wasn't that I was happy that Izzy was gone. I just knew that the vibration of my purrs would bring comfort. Mammy had been loyal to me the many times I had to go to Denis the Vet. It was my turn now.

☼

Sid

After Izzy passed I could see her lying on the end of Mammy's bed like she used to. Mammy would sit straight up in the bed and say, "Is that you, Izzy?" I think she could feel the weight of her on her foot and see the indentation in the bed. After a while Izzy stopped visiting and I knew she was gone for good. I know we will be together again in the Golden Field but to this day I still miss her.

☼

Harry Three Paws

After Izzy got killed, Mammy got very nervous about us being out, especially at night. She started keeping us in at night and I didn't like this at all. Like I've said, I am my own cat. I am independent. I have places to go and people to see. So Mammy and I began a cat-and-mouse game. I would hide outside until after dark. She would have to come out into the back laneway in hail, rain or snow and call me. She would try to cajole me to come in. Sometimes she bribed me with chicken. Sometimes she grabbed me and stuffed me inside the back door, and sometimes Sid got out past her as she was bringing me in. She muttered that it was like herding mice.

She even got into cahoots with the neighbours. There I would be, sitting up like royalty in Mona's house with the best seat in front of the fire, being admired as the Only Cat, and Mona's phone would make a noise. Then Mammy would turn up and I would be handed over like a furry parcel. The only consolation was that she always threw bits of chicken down the hallway for me to chase when we got home. She called it my Disturbance Money. Eventually she figured out that I love catnip and would bring a catnip toy out to lure me in. I found it hard resist it so it worked most of the time.

In the morning time, before we were released to the wild, Mammy would whisper an invocation to Archangel Michael to keep us all safe, while I muttered "Yeah, yeah, let me out of this hellhole immediately. I have been held hostage all night and need to secure my territory." And off I would go to patrol my patch.

☼

Tilly

When I got out of the cage I had to stay in the house for three weeks so that I would get used to the energy of the place. I took over the cat bed that had the number one view of the front of the house so that I could assess the Mouse and Bird population. I can't help it; when a bird flies past I instinctively tense to try to catch it. The movement of prey triggers a reaction from my brain. I come from a long line of cats whose survival depended on catching their food. I have no interest in eating plants, except grass. We cats eat grass in order to make us throw up fur balls. The Orange Woman only eats plants and grass and things like that. Sometimes she cooks chicken for us but I can tell she doesn't like it from the way her nose scrunches up.

When I was finally let out, I followed Sid to learn where the perimeter of our territory is. But Sid is a Man Cat, and he always goes further than I want to. Mind you, it's no hardship to me to follow his cute tail and posterior as he goes on patrol. He was not pleased that the Orange Woman had brought me home but I am a strong pussycat and I guessed that he would come around in time.

The Orange Woman calls him "My beautiful boy!" in a honey voice that sounds like a caress. She also calls him the Captain of the Furry Ship. Then she says she needs to get out more. I wouldn't say that Sid and I are friends exactly but we enjoy rough and tumble especially when the moon is full. I chase Sid up the stairs and then he chases me down the stairs. It's quite surprising how loud we can be.

Harry and I don't get on at all really but there is one amusing thing that he does which is to leap in the air and do a back flip when the Orange Woman throws a piece of chicken down the hallway for him. It cracks her up every time. Sometimes she does it wrong and he sits there, staring at the piece of chicken with a sad look on his face. Then she has to pick it up and throw it for him again. The all-time record is that she threw it four times. Then she said she was going to get a life and he could take it or leave it. He took it. Eventually. He is a very sociable cat and has a strict routine of houses to visit at certain times. I have no interest in socialising. We have nothing in common except the fact that we are both cats and both tabbies. We look alike but we couldn't be more different. He often yowls at me and gives me a claw because he says I get too close. When the Orange Woman hears Harry yowling like this, she shouts sternly "What's going on there? Everyone behave themselves." And we subside.

Sid also says I get too close and gives me a box in the whiskers. The Orange Woman even says to me, "Tilly, get out of Sid's face or he's going to give you a swipe." She's right every time. I don't seem to be able to judge the right space. But I'm able to judge the space between me and a mouse perfectly. I brought some mouse gifts to the Orange Woman but bizarrely, she was very upset. Some of them were alive, and she gave them the healing energy and hustled them out of the house and over to the park before I could get around to the front of the house to catch them again.

Once a week, the Orange Woman puts on her orange clothes and goes away for a while. When she comes back, she peels off the orange clothes and puts them on the floor beside the washing machine. I sniff them out because they smell of the place I grew up in, the cattery. I roll around in them and it makes me feel good. It reminds me of how lucky I am to be here in a home, when there are so many cats with no homes. I don't think the Orange Woman planned to give me a forever home so we weren't all that close for a while. But I'm glad to be here, however it happened. And like Sid, she came around to liking me in the end. Sometimes she calls me Senorita Gonzales, apparently after a very fast cartoon mouse on the television called Speedy Gonzales. Even though he's a mouse and I'm a cat. Sometimes it's hard to figure humans out, isn't it?

I eventually learned that the Orange Woman was our Cat Mammy. I tried to show her my affection by jumping up on her stomach and I couldn't understand why she went "Ooof!" I know I am a substantial cat but even so, it was surprising when she doubled over and said, "Oh my God, Tilly, get off my stomach. You're a ton weight."

Being a feral cat, I had made sure to stock up for the winter and the lean times by eating my food, Sid's food, and Harry's food. But the lean times didn't come. All that happened was that my figure went from lean and mean to furry and rotund. "You're like a big lynx," Cat Mammy said, showing me a picture of one. The only difference was that his ears were funny at the tips and the tip of one of my ears is jagged.

When feral cats are neutered in Ireland, the vet cuts the tip of one ear off under anaesthetic so that people doing the Trap, Neuter and Return work will know who has already been neutered and who still needs to be done. All I remember about my feral colony was that there were many, many cats and kittens, no shelter and not enough food. I don't know why the tip of my ear is jagged. Maybe the vet was having a bad day. But it doesn't hurt and it gives me a bit of a pirate look so it's okay.

One night I decided that a good place to sleep would be on top of Cat Mammy's head. I heard on the radio that two thirds of a human's body heat goes out through their head so this seemed very logical to me. I settled down and Cat Mammy stirred. I sank my claws into her head to stop her from moving and she shot up in the bed with a shout. I could see the whites of her eyes. I catapulted off the bed myself with the fright. It was not a restful night. I'm still not sure what went wrong but I don't think I will try that again.

Chapter 5

The Queen of Sheba

Harry Three Paws

One day I came home from my travels and neighbourhood supervision to find Mammy carrying in another cat basket. My heart sank. This one was called Snowy and she said that he was just staying while he recovered from an operation. He stayed two months but thank heavens his day of departure did arrive and good riddance too.

I relaxed after that and let my guard down but a few months later I came home from my travels and neighbourhood supervision to find Mammy carrying in yet another cat basket. A black and white tuxedo cat emerged from it this time and I could see that this one had Mammy wrapped around her paw. You'd think she was the Queen of Sheba. She did this insanely cute thing of sitting on her hind paws and waving her front paws in the air like a human baby wanting to be picked up. It made me want to throw up fur balls. Her name was Felicity and she was an ordinary cat, not feral. She looked very like Izzy, and I didn't need to be a puss psychologist to see that Mammy was trying to create a new story with a better ending.

Mammy said that was it, no more permanent cats. Enough was enough. I threw my eyes to cat heaven and hopped out in disgust and protest on my three paws. Not only was I not an Only Cat, clearly I would never be an Only Cat in this joint. The place was full of bloody cats.

☼

Tilly

After two years Cat Mammy came home with another cat. She is a black and white tuxedo cat called Felicity. We didn't need another cat so I don't know why Cat Mammy brought her home. I don't like her at all. She loves people and is very friendly to them. She makes me look bad with my poor social skills and spatial awareness deficit. She stands up on her hind legs and waves her paws in the air and humans love it. It makes me very annoyed so sometimes I chase her just for the hell of it. Then Cat Mammy shouts "Tilly!" in a very stern voice so I stop. Cat Mammy doesn't like us fighting.

I sidle up to Mammy every day to be petted. I heard her saying that she wanted me to get used to being handled. I'm not sure how that is working out because the last time I had to go to Denis the Vet he had to put a pillow on top of me in the special wire basket

I was in, and inject me through the wire. Mammy muttered something to Denis about getting a dart gun with a telescopic sight for my next visit.

But nearly every day she lifts me up and plonks me on the sofa. When I was younger she used to wheel me around her head and say, "Look, Tilly, you're the first feral cat in space!" and I enjoyed it. Now she grunts when she lifts me and it seems my flying days are over. I suppose it's because she is getting older and weaker. I can't imagine why else it would be.

☼

Harry Three Paws

As you know we cats like to stretch a lot, it keeps us supple and lithe. Mammy likes to stretch too, and I don't know why but she calls it yoga. She has a special purple mat for stretching on. I get quite excited when I see this mat being unrolled because I love hiding under things and pouncing. One day Mammy was there, lying on her back and she didn't realise that I had burrowed underneath the mat. She rolled backwards to do a shoulder stand and nearly squashed me to death. I shot out and applied The Claw to her scalp in my own defence and she screamed and did an impressive sort of breakdance manoeuvre that brought her to her feet with her hair standing up more than usual. After that she was very wary of me when she unrolled that mat.

Mammy listens to a radio station that plays music from the last century. One evening she heard a song on the radio and started dancing around the kitchen waving the tea towel and giggling. She couldn't see the spirit of a black and white cat weaving in and out between her legs but I could. I will say this for Mammy though: for an unbelievably ancient human, she can move when she wants to.

☼

A few times some of the local children chased me and sneered at me. Once they caught me. They laughed at me because I couldn't get away from them and pulled my tail. I was very frightened and angry. I lashed out with The Claw and the one who was holding me was so surprised he let me go, but kicked me as I ran away and hurt my spine. I dragged myself home on my two front paws and Mammy was in tears when she saw me. She didn't know what had happened to me and it's just as well. She is very quiet but I know she has a protective fire inside and would have rescued me and wreaked havoc on my tormentors. I can see in her energy field that she has a big softness inside her for animals and wants to help and protect them. Of course, we had another visit to Denis the Vet, with more anti-inflammatory medicine which left me stoned again. Mammy said I have eyes like saucers when I'm on that stuff.

Sometimes I want to scratch under my chin on the right side but of course I can't because I am missing my back right leg. When Mammy sees me trying to do this, she scratches my chin for me. Nobody else does this for me. And although I eat mostly dried food, I like a little wet cat food every day. Mammy puts a teaspoon of wet food in my bowl and uses a sharp knife to puncture a cod liver oil capsule. Then she picks it up with pliers and squeezes it over the food. She says it's to ward off arthritis and I like the taste of it. My fur is lovely and shiny because of it, too.

When Mammy goes up or down stairs she pulls a string with feathers attached after her so that Felicity or Tilly can chase it. When Mammy looks at Felicity I see her heart opening with great tenderness. Sometimes she sits on the sofa reading and Felicity sleeps on her lap. I am not jealous because I am not a Lap Cat. I am a Warrior Cat. Occasionally I do sit on Mammy's lap if I want some Reiki energy healing for my spine but I don't tell many people about that as it would affect my street credibility.

I have learned the value of kindness by its absence and its presence. The small things matter. It's the small things that make us who we are.

☼

As I have said, Tilly is a mad feral cat. She's like a wild animal. In fact, she IS a wild animal and her reactions are lightning-fast and instinctive. She also must have missed the day in Cat School where they explained about the importance of personal boundaries because she is always getting it wrong. From us other cats, she gets a hiss and a claw when she gets too close.

One day Mammy fell asleep on the sofa and Tilly perched on the back cushions, purring above her head like a UFO - an Unexploded Furry Ordinance. You wouldn't have to be psychic to see what was likely to happen next. My mind raced as I planned to run around to Niall and miaow loudly at him, like Lassie warning that Timmy had fallen into the well. "Follow me, Niall! Call an ambulance!"

Mammy opened her eyes and yawned. Tilly's tail hung down over the back of the sofa and Mammy patted it absentmindedly. I saw the realisation dawn on her as to who was sitting on her head and she froze. I held my breath. I could see the wheels turning in her head. Ever so slowly, she reached for a feather on the sofa and picked it up, saying "Look Tilly!" in a squeaky voice as she twitched it. Tilly, being a total hunter, was transfixed by the feather and pounced to secure it. Normally Mammy would use a ten foot long string to safeguard her skin but it was an emergency. She sustained scratches but at least she was alive to tell the tale.

CHAPTER 6

Craziness Abounds

Felicity

I was born lucky. Of all the gardens I could have wandered into, I walked into the one belonging to the daughter of Helen, who runs the cattery in Dog's Aid. That's where I ended up. They were very nice to me there. I wasn't much more than a kitten myself but I was already pregnant. The vet said I was last year's kitten, so I was very young. Whatever he did, when I left the vet's I had a scar on my belly but no kittens inside. I felt relieved because I could hardly look after myself, never mind kittens. A really nice woman in the cattery called Rita named me Felicity. She said I looked like the cat on the Felix tins only he was a boy and I am a girl. My name means

Happiness and it was well chosen because I am a happy-go-lucky cat. One day a woman came into the cattery. Now I am no arbiter of sartorial elegance but this woman was dressed in an appalling orange outfit. I stood on my hind legs and waved my front paws at her. That's all it took. She was smitten. When she took me home with her she said my full name was Felicity Sophia. Sophia means "wisdom" in Greek. Happy Wisdom! I quite like the ring of it myself.

When I arrived in my new home there were already three cats living there. Sid was the Top Cat. He was not happy with the arrival of a new cat, even less when he saw what I looked like. It turned out that I looked quite like his friend Izzy who had been killed by a car six months earlier. Tilly was a feral cat who glared at me. Harry Three Paws was my hero even though he ignored me. I followed him everywhere when I was younger and tried to copy everything he did.

Even though I have four legs and he only has three, in many ways he is more nimble than I was. People always think cats have great coordination but I don't. I can't judge how far it is to jump up on a table, for instance, and I frequently fall short or fall off things. One day I tried to jump up on the toilet seat and I fell into the toilet bowl. It was yukky. Tilly sniggered but Mammy just said, "Oh for God's sake!" and fished me out. Then she washed me and dried me. So while it was a bit embarrassing, it was nice to be coddled. I like being coddled.

I like playing and every evening at about 7 pm I have my Crazy Hour. My eyes get very wide and I run around like a lunatic.

Sometimes Mammy pulls a string with a feather on the end of it around for me. I chase it and jump around the place. It makes Mammy giggle. Tilly pounces on it with her big ham fisted paw the size of a saucer and that's the end of the game. No feather is going to escape from that one, I can tell you. She may be a super hunter but she doesn't understand that if you don't let go of the feather that is the end of the game. Holding on just doesn't work.

I learned from Harry about how to visit other families. I sometimes visit Niall and Mary although Harry doesn't encourage me. They are clearly his people, and not mine. Sometimes I waltz into Mona's house to have a look around, and leave again. Mona said to Mammy that I was like the Queen, inviting myself in for a viewing. There are other nice neighbours called Margaret and Jerry and I also visit them and allow them to admire me. In the summertime, Harry and I lie on the top of Christine's car because it has a soft top and it gets nice and warm. One day Christine and Peter were going somewhere and Christine said, "What's that noise?" and she looked around and there I was, sitting up in the middle of the back seat. I thought we were off for a jaunt. I thought it was normal. It was news to me that I wasn't allowed to go with them but there you go.

☼

Sid

Mammy's friend Sue came to stay for a short visit. Like Mammy, she only eats weeds and grassy things. I will say, however, that for two old people they look pretty healthy. Anyway, Sue is a Cat Person. I could see that straight away because she had cat hairs on her clothes when she arrived. One evening Mammy was going out and she asked Sue to get me in before dark if she could. I took advantage of Mammy's absence to stay out longer than usual. When I did come back, I stayed on the wall for a while. As I am jet black and it was already dark, of course Sue couldn't see me. But I was quite puzzled as to why she was talking to a black rubbish bag outside the back door, trying to persuade it to come in, while I was out in the cold. Humans are strange creatures.

☼

Harry Three Paws

Next door different people come and go, moving in and moving out. They don't seem to stay in the house very long. One lot of people who lived there for a while had a little boy who had a big toy tractor. He used to leave it out on the front lawn and I loved sitting up on the seat. Niall seemed to think it was really funny and took a photo of me on the tractor. Mammy said I should be on Top Gear.

One day I supervised Mammy as she took an unusual chair out of the car. The chair had wheels and she said she was loaning it to a neighbour. I hopped up on the seat and off we went. We passed a stranger on the way and his eyes were out on stalks. Mammy said that he had probably never seen a three legged cat in a wheelchair before and maybe he thought this was my normal mode of perambulation, or maybe he was like herself and needed to get out a bit more.

When Mammy goes away, Emma comes to stay with us and mind us. We are all delighted with this as we see it as a great opportunity to stay out late. I make myself scarce as darkness approaches and of course, with my grey and chocolate tabby stripes, I am nearly invisible. I can hear Emma calling me but I ignore her.

Recently I was in Niall and Mary's and I heard their doorbell. Emma was asking them if they had seen me but they hadn't. An hour later, Niall came into the front sitting room and there I was. I had managed to slip past him when a visitor came and was disporting myself on the couch. Emma came and carried me home. Another night, she had seized me and I was indoors but Felicity was still at large. Emma started running after Felicity, who thought it was a great game. The new Brazilian neighbours have taken Felicity to their hearts. So there were four Brazilians running around the neighbourhood after Felicity. Emma grabbed a pair of Mammy's gardening clogs to join in the chase, and put one foot in and then screamed loudly. It seems that either Tilly or Felicity had peed in one of the clogs. It certainly wasn't one of us Men Cats. Not our thing.

☼

Felicity

Mammy often says that Helen who runs the cattery is the bee's knees and the cat's pyjamas. I've never seen a bee's knee so I am not sure about that. With regard to pyjamas, last Christmas Mammy got into the festive spirit and bought a Santy outfit for Harry. It was a red coat with a cute tassel on top of the hood. She tried to put it on him but it didn't go down well. Harry was outraged at this affront to his dignity and deployed the Ninja Claw. I had to look away. It was amazing that one three legged cat could spill so much human blood. Mammy retreated, chastened, to dress her wounds. I don't think she will be doing that again soon.

In the wintertime, Mammy often puts a sheet or duvet cover on the banister to air it out. I love hiding underneath it and then jumping out and attacking someone. I don't mind who it is. One day she was downstairs in the kitchen when I was rolling around Playing Attack of the Killer Duvet Cover when my claws got stuck in the fabric. I made a sound and Mammy rushed to the bottom of the stairs just in time to see me abseiling the whole way down attached to the duvet cover. I landed with a plop on the carpet. I can honestly say I have never heard Mammy laugh so much. "The look on your face, Felicity" she chortled. The Gods must have been looking after me that it was not captured on film. Even though the internet was obviously invented for cat videos, they are not always complimentary to us cats. Sometimes we even look foolish. I did an emergency shoulder lick to restore my dignity and left the scene.

About six months ago something fantastic happened. A big load of new people moved into the house across the road. One of them, Eduardo, started giving me treats. It turned out that he and his wife Karina had a cat in their home country that looked like me. So I think Mammy got me because I looked like Izzy and I think Eduardo gives me treats because I look like his cat, Beans. Mammy says that Eduardo is from Brazil, where the nuts come from. All the people in Eduardo's house are nice to me. Either Mammy comes over to collect me from my sleepovers or Eduardo carries me back home. I get ferried around the place every day. I hardly have to walk at all. It's great.

Mammy and Sid talk to each other a lot. He goes "Mang," and she goes "Mang" back to him. Then he goes "Aow" and she goes "Aow." You get the picture. It's a primitive form of communication but they seem happy with it. If you are reading this book, then you are presumably a Cat Person and you know that we cats only Miaow to communicate with humans. In fact, we invented the Audible Miaow for interspecies communication in order to upgrade our food, treats and toys. I wouldn't say Mammy is fluent in Cat. Sometimes Sid goes "Wow a wow wow" and she says, "I don't care if there is a full moon, you're not getting out until tomorrow morning." Other times he goes "Aaaow" and she says "More food Sid?" but that is about as good as it gets. When he is out in the back laneway and it's getting dark, she sends him a signal. She sends energy from her heart, her forehead and above her head to connect with him and tell him to come home. Sometimes it takes him a while but he always turns up. I know Mammy loves me but Sid seems extra special to her. I don't know whether it's because he's been here the longest or what.

It's harder for her to get Harry inside. Sometimes the doorbell rings and Niall or Mona deliver Harry. Between Eduardo, Niall and Mona it's like a Cat Delivery Service. Harry always wants to be out longer than everyone else. He won't come in when he is called. Mammy goes out Harry hunting with a torch and a black sock full of catnip.

Harry sits up on Mona's wall. Sometimes he comes within reach and she grabs him by the scruff and lifts him down. Funny enough, he doesn't seem to mind and actually starts purring. I guess maybe he is testing her to see does she love him enough to come after him. Or maybe he doesn't want to admit that his back is tired and he would like to rest, but if Mammy grabs him, well that's okay. He has to come inside and rest then. When his back gets sore he jumps up on her knee for some healing. Otherwise he ignores her. Normal cat stuff.

Sometimes when it's rainy and dark out Mammy will make a fire and sit in front of it reading. One night Sid was at her feet, Tilly on her lower legs, Harry on her knee and I was above her head on the arm of the sofa. Mammy said she was in Cat Nirvana. I'm not sure what that is but she sounded happy about it.

She says I have a special talent for making sure that my fur balls are always thrown up on a mat or carpet, never on the wooden floor. I don't know what her problem is. What difference does it make? When a fur ball needs to come out, it needs to come out. Better out than in, is my motto.

Usually I steer clear of Tilly who is very large and unpredictable. But when my Crazy Hour arrives, I get a rush of adrenalin and I often chase her. Her ears flatten and she runs away from me. Mam shouts at me and gives me a time out in the hall but it's worth it.

In the morning time, the others all race out to meet the day but I take my time. I like to have a lie in. Mammy makes sure I am covered by a small fleece blanket in the wintertime. She brings me breakfast in bed, wherever I have decided to sleep.

I suspect that either Mammy is a bit deaf or has the madness in the head, because she often scoops me up and puts me next to her ear. I purr away and she laughs. I suppose she could be BOTH deaf and mad. She says that the vibrations of a cat's purr are very healing. Not for deafness or madness in the head, obviously.

☼

Harry Three Paws

In the wintertime, Mammy lights the fire and stretches out in front of it. Well, she tries to, but not very successfully. Sometimes I am on her knee, Sid is at her right side, Tilly at her feet and Felicity above her head. There isn't room to swing a cat. Some evenings my back gets sore from the day's work patrolling my neighbourhood so I settle down and absorb some nice warm healing vibes for my spine. Mammy puts her hand over the place where my leg used to be and I can feel the heat and the love. "You are much more than your missing leg, Harry," she often says. "You are an Important Community Cat."

Every evening, when Mammy has finally rounded us all up, she locks the door for the night and thanks the angels for looking after us. Before she goes to bed, she comes to each one of us in turn and whispers a special word in each person's ear. She kisses me on the head and tells me that I am a beautiful boy and that she will love me forever. I believe her now.

In the wintertime she tucks a small, warm, soft fleece blanket around me. It feels nice. When I was younger I gave her The Claw for doing this. But now that I am older and wiser, I let her do it and sometimes I even purr. She always sounds so surprised to hear me purr, she says "Harry! You're purring!" She tucks in Felicity and Sid with small blankets too, but just pats Tilly on the head as tucking her in would result in hospitalisation.

Life did not turn out as I had hoped or expected and this home is not perfect. I guess I have accepted now that I will never be an Only Cat here. I am, however, The Only Three Legged Cat here. One of my dreams did come true, though: I am loved and cherished. This time it's for who I am, leg or no leg. This time it's for real. And that is enough.

Epilogue

Gannet

I was in the Golden Field when a shower of rose petals fell on me. I purred because I knew straight away that they came from Mammy and that I lived on in her heart. One day I visited her in the garden when she was hanging out washing with my friend Peg. She straightened my grave marker and whispered "I know you forgive me for holding on to you too long and for all the mistakes I made, Gan. I love you always and forever." I was delighted. Part Three of my life's mission was now complete: to teach Mammy about self-forgiveness.

☼

The man with the brightest of bright blue eyes felt light-hearted and peaceful as he walked towards the Golden Field. He could hear birds singing, especially robins, his favourite. The sun shone in the blue sky and the temperature was just perfect. The Field had a meadow with brightly coloured flowers in it. They smelled beautiful. He heard a sound and looked behind him. A cat miaowed at him and then twined in and out through his ankles. "Ah there you are, Puss." He leaned down to pet the cat and she purred loudly to this nice man who somehow seemed so familiar. As he left the Field he was closely followed by the black tuxedo cat, tail straight up in the air.

End Notes

Thank you very much for reading this book. I hope you have enjoyed it. I would really appreciate if you could take the time to put an honest review of it on Amazon.com or Goodreads.com

☼

About the Author

Marese Hickey has done aerobatics in a vintage Tiger Moth in New Zealand, meditated in Tibet, and has swum with wild dolphins in the Bahamas. She is an energy healer, holistic therapist and former nurse. She has worked as a clinical hypnotherapist for nineteen years. Marese is an animal healer and servant to four cats.

☼

Contact

www.maresehickey.com

Facebook @maresehickeywriter

Twitter @maresehickey1

Instagram https://www.instagram.com/maresehickey

Also by Marese Hickey

How to Love Yourself in Less than 50 Years

The Power of Inner Change for Outer Results EBook Series

Vol. 1 Letting Go of the Past

Vol. 2 Mind Direction

Vol. 3 Yes to Life

Dog's Aid Animal Sanctuary

Dog's Aid is a no-kill rescue centre in Dublin, Ireland, which aims to rescue, rehabilitate and rehome animals. It is run entirely by volunteers. Donations are much appreciated and the money is all spent on the animals.

For more information or to donate, see www.dogsaid.ie

Acknowledgements

To my friends and editorial team - thank you so much for your help, feedback and friendship: Emma Champ, Sue Smith, Veron Bennett and Dolores O'Malley.

Printed in Great Britain
by Amazon